EXPERT ADVISOR AND FOREX TRADING STRATEGIES

Take Your Expert Advisor and Forex Trading

To The Next Level

WAYNE WALKER

Table of Contents

INTRODUCTION

Τhis book will expand your trading knowledge as we dive deep into the world of programmed trading and advanced strategies for both forex and equities. The goal of my writing is to provide you with practical and useful trading information. There are no wild and unbelievable stories which is often what you and other readers will encounter in finance literature. I prefer to share interesting things that I have experienced while trading and provide an insight into how things really work.

As an investor or trader you will at some point come across online posts which state "best break out strategy." You will also find research articles and books explaining the average returns of various strategies and providing statistics on them. Now what if you ask yourself, "do they work?" and you then begin the testing process. As a trader it's important to know how the simulated results are calculated and you will also need them be as precise as possible. Let us proceed to test some different strategies and trading systems.

The format of the first three chapters are in the form of a trade adventure where a strategy will be introduced, tested, and finally refined.

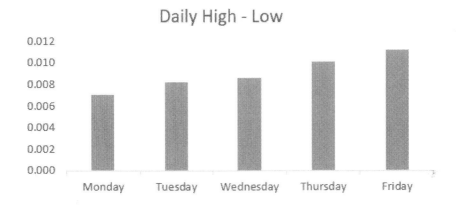

Daily High - Low

CHAPTER 1:
The Day Of The Week Anomaly

R esearch has shown that stocks and other markets tend to move more on Fridays than Mondays. To test this we have back data from 2001-2016. We will use an approximately 80/20 split where 80% will be in sample and the remainder out of sample.

Note: In Sample - Out of Sample: It is statistics speak which in most cases means "using past data to make forecasts of the future". "In sample" refers to the data that you have and "out of sample" to the data you don't have but want to forecast or estimate.

The Signal

To begin we have the issue with daylight savings time, which requires that we offset the time settings. Forex is the main market for our test. There was a little debate on which time of the day would be optimal for the trade, should we stick to the European, New York or the Asian session close. To keep things relatively simple we will just buy on the open of the day and hold the positions to the open of the next day.

The Day of the week effect for Friday, we buy on Friday 00.00 and sell 00.00 on Monday. This obligates that we take into account the gap (weekend), but we do not consider it a big issue. Time should also not be a significant factor because the real volatility triggers are when the market is open. Therefore, if we don't close Friday evening but hold until Monday it will not have a noticeable impact because the market does not move when it is closed.

Data

Our in-sample time period is 01.01.2001-31.12.2011 and out of sample time period is 01.01.2012-01.06.2016. The instrument that we will trade is EURUSD.

Basic Strategy

We will begin with just the basic strategy without any changes of parameters. The strategy is buy on the first tick after 00.00 Friday and sell the first price move on Monday (00.00). We had some problems with the time because of daylight savings time therefore we decided to just buy on first tick of Friday. This is something different from what has been provided by previous studies using excel or any other program measuring the average price change from the day of open to close (next day open). We are using tick data and a simulator that is simulating the real trading environment to get our result as precise as possible.

Note: Tick: A tick is a measure of the minimum upward or downward movement in the price of a security. A tick can also refer to the change in the price of a security from trade to trade.

First Results

To begin we did not include any stop-loss or take profit, just ran it. We also did not make any other adjustments on the strategy our testing period was 01.01-2005 to 26.08.2016.

The results were the following:

Results	
Average profit	-1.57
Sum profit	-897.84
Winning trade	297
Total trades	572
Standard dev	96.55
Relnumber	-0.39

They were disappointing, the total profit was -897. Clearly, the basic strategy is in need of some fine-tuning to improve our results.

Adding Trend Filter Exponential Moving Average

We applied the trend filter 20 EMA, 60 EMA, and 100 EMA. An Exponential Moving Average (EMA) is a type of moving average that is similar to a Simple Moving Average, except that more weight is given to the latest data. It is also known as the Exponentially Weighted Moving Average. This type of moving average reacts faster to recent price changes than a Simple Moving Average. For some this may appear random but this filter was chosen because of the number of days it counts.

20 EMA = 20 trading days in a month
60 EMA = 60 trading days equals three months
100 EMA = 100 trading days equals five months

Trend filter: 20EMA>60EMA>100EMA

The chart illustrates this trend filter:

You can see that it only opens trades when the 20 EMA (in green) is above 60 EMA (in yellow) and 60 EMA is above 100 EMA (in red). I could have only used 20 EMA>100 EMA but that would have had more volatility or false entry signals. I wanted both the long term (60 EMA>100 EMA) and short term (20 EMA>60 EMA) trends to be up.

We got following results:

	Average profit	Sum profit	Winning trade	Total trades	Standard dev	Reinumber
The Basic Strategy	-2	-898	297	572	97	-0.39
20EMA>60EMA>100EMA	6	1832	178	322	86	1.19
20EMA<60EMA<100EMA	-12	-1831	68	147	103	-1.47

To compare two or more systems it is not enough to only examine the profits. This is because profit is only one of the indicators. What is equally important is the number of trades and volatility. It does not make sense to have one system with just one big or a few profitable trades and many losses. Those few profitable trades could be random, they could be a Black Swan which most likely will not repeat in the future, therefore we don't want too much variance. The formula for that term is:

$$Rel = \frac{\text{Average profit}}{\text{Standard deviation of profit}} * \sqrt{\# \ of \ trades}$$

You can typically expect better returns from a strategy with many trades than one with only a few. To summarize, the higher the Rel number the better the trading system.

One thing we can conclude is that by applying the filter for uptrend we have better returns than the basic strategy. The other is that this strategy works better in uptrend market than in downtrend, we had negative returns in a down market. We had greater Rel number with a trend filter.

Volatility Filter

Our opinion is that volatility is also an important indicator. Volatility is constantly changing so comparing recent volatility will also make sense. We will compare the 10 days average range to the 1 day average range. This will allow us to see excess volatility and the opposite. Using these settings is the same as saying today's volatility compared to the average volatility of last 10 trading days (two weeks).

We got following results:

	Average profit	Sum profit	Winning trade	Total trades	Standard dev	Relnumber
The Basic Strategy	-2	-898	297	572	97	-0.39
20EMA>60EMA>100EMA	6	1832	178	322	86	1.19
20EMA<60EMA<100EMA	-12	-1831	68	147	103	-1.47
ATR(1)>ATR(10)	-2	-356.74	73	143	82	-0.4
ATR(1)<ATR(10)	12	2188.62	105	179	88	1.9

The results showed that **excess volatility** on Thursdays destroys this strategy, meaning if the range on the Thursday before is above the last two weeks volatility it's bad for the strategy. However, if the opposite is true, the range is less than the last ten days average range we will make money with this strategy. If you don't get it right away it will become clearer. For now just know it's clear that this strategy works well when there is an **uptrend** and **volatility is less** than the previous two weeks. As an investor or trader you will buy when you see that EURUSD is in uptrend both in short and long term. We also saw that we improved the Rel number, we made fewer trades but increased profits. A decrease in volatility increased our Rel number, which is good. Remember we do not want to gamble, we only want to trade when it is appropriate. Our Rel number has improved from 1.19 to 1.9.

Gambling or Investing With Calculated Risk = Stop-loss!

I personally avoid trading without a stop-loss, I need to know what I'm risking on each particular trade. Using my personal formula I figured that the right stop-loss for this strategy is 50 pips. The results:

Introducing stop-loss decreases the volatility. You can see that we improved the Rel number and decreased the number of winning trades. The increase in Rel number means that there were several trades which moved more than 50 pips against us before they went into profit again. This for me is similar to gambling, I would rather exclude such trades and set a stop-loss at 50 pips.

Position Sizing and Fixed % Per Trade

Have you ever executed a trade without considering that if you lose above a fixed percent of your equity you should close the trade? In trading this not recommended, I never open a trade without calculating the risk. We will now move onto the concept of a fixed percent trade. This is where the lot size will be a function of our stop-loss and a risk tolerance of 1%. You take more risk when your equity increases and take less when your equity decreases.

With position sizing we increased our overall profit, but we also increased the volatility in our equity curve, so our Rel number decreased a bit. I would rather include position sizing than to rely on higher Rel number.

	Average profit	Sum profit	Winning trade	Total trades	Standard dev	Relnumber
The Basic Strategy	-2	-898	297	572	97	-0.39
20EMA>60EMA>100EMA	6	1832	178	322	86	1.19
20EMA<60EMA<100EMA	-12	-1831	68	147	103	-1.47
ATR(1)>ATR(10)	-2	-356.74	73	143	82	-0.4
ATR(1)<ATR(10)	12	2188.62	105	179	88	1.9
50 pips SL	11	2024.08	87	179	66	2.3
Position sizing	13	2280	85	179	77	2.22

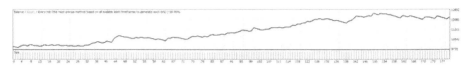

Equity curve in sample with position sizing

Out of Sample Test

We did out of sample test in the period 01.01.2012–01.08.2016

	Average profit	Sum profit	Winning trade	Total trades	Standard dev	Relnumber
The Basic Strategy	-2	-898	297	572	97	-0.39
20EMA>60EMA>100EMA	6	1832	178	322	86	1.19
20EMA<60EMA<100EMA	-12	-1831	68	147	103	-1.47
ATR(1)>ATR(10)	-2	-356.74	73	143	82	-0.4
ATR(1)<ATR(10)	12	2188.62	105	179	88	1.9
50 pips SL	11	2024.08	87	179	66	2.3
Position sizing	13	2280	85	179	77	2.22
Out of sample	5	189	19	37	49	1

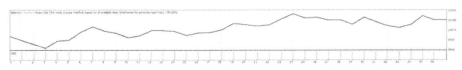

Equity curve out of sample

The results were not so promising we got sum profit of 189, the start equity was 10,000 USD so this equals a 1.89 % return. We also got a smaller Rel number which is not so good. The maximum drawdown received of 289 was way above the sum profit. Obviously, I was unsatisfied with these results.

Summary

We have taken several steps to improve the Day of The Week strategy. What we can say for sure is that you will not make any money when you include transaction cost in the basic strategy. This strategy works best in uptrend market. As an experienced trader I believe the timeframe might be the problem. The strategy could have been more profitable but we were not giving it enough time. The stop-loss on 50 pips is enough, but on the other side we closed our trade on Monday whatever the results were. There is a need of further refinement. We will keep the same entry strategy but the trade management needs to be different. When making trades with this we will need to include a take profit function of the weekly volatility or trailing stop. These needed improvements will be seen in the next chapters.

CHAPTER 2:
First Refinement:
Day of The Week Effect Strategy

We move forward to make our first adjustment to the Day of The Week Effect strategy from the last chapter. What I will point to as the weakness with the Day of The Week Effect is the traditional way to trade it. This weakness is to close the trade on Monday morning because you are taking some risk even when you are using a stop-loss. However, if you are not giving the trade enough time then you will not get the maximum possible profit. A simple but respected rule of trading is to "cut your losses and let your profits run."

After examining the strategy, I realized that it only made money because it had some good trades that moved 300-400 pips during one day. Unfortunately, this is infrequent and includes many drawdowns that I would prefer not to have in my portfolio. We will now see the difference in equity using some different ways to manage the trade, our entry signal remains the same. You will also see why it is important to include volatility in the planning.

Method

Using the same trading signal, but on Friday we open with 20EMA>60EMA (we have excluded the 100 EMA this time). Lot size will be 0.1 and account starting balance of 10,000 USD. The closing statement of Monday is removed and just have a stop-loss and take-profit. We split the data, in sample and out of sample. In sample we will optimize the different parameters and then perform an out of sample test to see whether or not the optimized strategy works well. We also increase the range of our in sample data 01.01.1990-01.01.2012. We will use a tight stop-loss, trailing stop and breakeven, we called this method *No Vols* because we will not include volatility in any of the tests.

Stop-Loss and Take Profit

Our strategy optimized the stop-loss and take-profit between 100 - 600 to see whether the results hold. It got an optimal stop-loss of 400 and take profit of 600. We received total profit of 86,413 and Rel number of 7.09 which we yet can't compare because in this test we had included an additional 11 years of prior data. It is necessary to combine this with other trade management methods and see which one is the best to manage after a trade has been executed. What we can compare is the average profit, it has increased to 138, where it wasn't more than 2,2 in the earlier test, just because we allowed our trade to run longer.

Methode	Average profit	Sum profit	Total # of trades	Winning # of Trades	Standard deviation of profit	Rel #
Only SL & TP	138 $	86,413	357	626	486.8007082	7.09

Graph showing equity with just stop-loss and take-profit. Here and on other graphs SL=Stop Loss and TP=Take-profit

Stop-loss, Take-profit and Break-even

Most traders are familiar with break-even. This is where you amend your stops when the market has moved a certain amount in your favor, this was included in our strategy. Break-even is good to have because if you don't use one, there is a risk that after having a profit you end the trade with a loss. We saw 71,480 USD profit and 6,99 of Rel number, a bit smaller than without use of break-even. It decreased the volatility in the equity curve, but also decreased the profit, meaning sometimes we were stopped out because we had changed our stop-loss to break-even, so this is a trade-off between risk/reward, you decrease your risk, you also get less return.

Methode	Average profit	Sum profit	Total # of trades	Winning # of Trades	Standard deviation of profit	Rel #
Only SL & TP	138 $	86,413	357	626	487	7.09
SL & TP & Breakeven	114 $	71,480	428	626	408	6.99

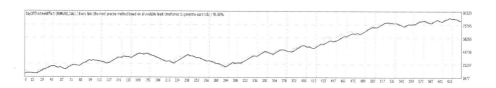

Graph showing equity with also break-even function we got a bit smoother equity curve

Stop-loss and Trailing stop

In this strategy we used Moving Averages, we were placing trades when the market was in an uptrend. It is important for you to remember the trader saying, "cut your losses and let your profit run." It's correct to have a stop-loss, but a predefined take profit will limit our profits in an uptrend because we don't know exactly how high it will go. Therefore we had to exclude the take profit and instead include a trailing stop function. We have increased our average profit to 350 per trade, increased our profits to 213,636 and our Rel number to 9.89. When we included the break-even function in it we only got 151,194 profit and 8.20 Rel number which was lower than what we received with using only a stop-loss and trailing stop. I will not include the break-even function in the future for this strategy. We will trail the stop below recent higher lows.

Methode	Average profit		Sum profit	Total # of trades	Winning # of Trades	Standard deviation of profit	Rel #
Only SL & TP	138	$	86,413	357	626	487	7.09
SL & TP & Breakeven	114	$	71,480	428	626	408	6.99
SL & TP & Trailingstop	350	$	213,636	305	610	875	9.89
SL & TP & Breakeven & Trailingstop	242	$	151,194	425	626	737	8.20

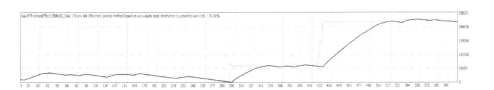

Graph showing equity with just only stop-loss and trailing stop function

Graph showing equity with just only stop-loss, break-even and trailing-stop function

Out of Sample Test

The out of sample test period was 01.01.2012–01.09.2016. We experienced disappointing results, to be more direct, we lost all of our trading capital and got stopped out. As traders we want to know if our results will be valid in the future. We know that there are different ways to manage trades that will improve our results.

Volatility is very important, EURUSD had been trading in a range since 2014, therefore you should not use stop-loss and take profit optimized in the period before it, none of the trade management tools are dynamic or valid without taking an account of the volatility.

Methode	Average profit	Sum profit	Total # of trades	Winning # of Trades	Standard deviation of profit	Rel #
Only SL & TP	138 $	86,413	357	626	487	7.09
SL & TP & Breakeven	114 $	71,480	428	626	408	6.99
SL & TP & Trailingstop	350 $	213,636	305	610	875	9.89
SL & TP & Breakeven & Trailingstop	242 $	151,194	425	626	737	8.20
Out of Sample	-127 $	(9,770)	22	77	216	-5.16

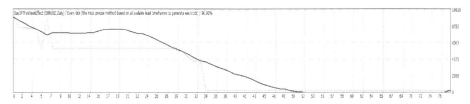

Graph showing equity out of sample test results

Summary

We showed the importance of different trade management styles and the importance of volatility in our strategy. The current market could be different from the market we had during our testing period. EURUSD was our test pair and in the background, 2013, the American and European stock markets were at all-time highs, people were waiting for a crash or an excuse for this currency pair to get out of the continuation pattern. The pair had been trading within a tight range and market players wanted a breakout to either the up or downside.

It is important to keep in mind that your strategy will fail if you don't account for the volatility in the market. If you are day trading and use a stop-loss of 20 pips and a take profit of 100 pips but you see that on average the daily range has been 60 pips, you will never hit your take profit. If you have a trend strategy you will never achieve the full potential of the trade if you just use take profit, it's much better to trail the stop below the recent high or low. You can see from the equity curve graph where we only had a stop-loss and trailing stop in the first half of the trade we did not gain much profits. This is because at that time the range was not as wide. Therefore using just take profit and stop-loss will not deliver optimal results. One alternative is to reoptimize the parameters each month using the previous year or quarterly data. I prefer to use volatility based parameters.

CHAPTER 3:
Day of The Week Effect: Introducing Volatility

I n the previous chapters we have focused on the Day of The Week Effect anomaly and how it can be improved. We will continue to enhance the strategy by introducing volatility. Any trader will tell you that volatility is dynamic, it is constantly changing, sometimes we have excess volatility other times we have a contraction. If you optimize your strategy when the market has excess volatility and then at trade execution time there is a decrease in volatility you most likely will not hit your take-profit level. What you will instead experience is that your stops are frequently hit. It is important that your risk and reward levels are a function of current market volatility. Right before Brexit, for example, GBPUSD moved a lot more than its normal price movement pattern. We saw excess volatility because there were numerous conflicting and often confusing news reports before the last vote. If you as a day trader had placed a trade with a 20 pips stop-loss, you would have often experienced that your trade would hit the stop-loss and then quickly reverse after hitting it. We showed earlier how poor the results can be when we did not calculate for the volatility. Now I will show the difference of when you include volatility in your trade management.

Method

Keeping our Day of The Week Effect strategy, we will open the trade on the first tick on Friday. The pair testes is the same as used in the previous examples, EURUSD. Our in sample test period is 01.01.1990–01.01.2012. The starting balance will be 10,000 USD and amount per trade will be 0.1 lot. We will implement one change in our entry signal compared to our last trial. Earlier we mentioned that this strategy is a trend strategy, in other words, we buy if the trend is up. This applies to both long and short-term trends. As traders we know that this can also give us many stop-loss executions if the market overshoots. If we just enter and buy at the market price it will be in a range and this normally gives a poor risk-reward ratio to the latest top. Therefore it is better to buy on pullbacks because then you have more of a distance to the previous top, and an improved risk-reward. The execution is the following: the long-term trend 20 our EMA is above the 60 EMA, however the shorter term trend the 5 EMA is below our 20 EMA. It's Friday, we opened the trade with our settings. We did not buy blindly, **but** on the pullback as experienced traders like to do. We will have fewer trades but this is good.

Dynamic Stop-loss and Take-profit

We adjusted our stop-loss and take-profit as functions of the current volatility. This implies that it will adjust according to the current volatility and then we optimized the different parameters. We received the following results:

Method	Average profit	Sum Profit	# of winning trades	# of total trades	Standard deviation	Rel number
SL & TP	26.0	4497	98	173	234	1.46

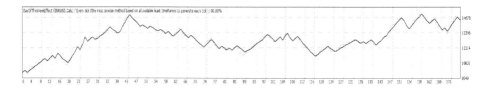

Graph showing equity curve by only using volatility stop-loss and take-profit.

We got total profit 4,497 during test period and Rel number for 1.46 and average profit of 26.

Dynamic Stop-Loss, Take-Profit and Break-Even

We will now introduce a break-even which will be a function of the current volatility and with this we increased the average profit to 33.9, sum profit to 5,687 and Rel number to 2.05. There was decreased volatility in the equity curve, and also some of our losing trades become winning trades by adding break-even. Using this function we also locked in some profit above our entry price.

Method	Average profit	Sum Profit	# of winning trades	# of total trades	Standard deviation	Rel number
SL & TP	26.0	4497	98	173	234	1.46
SL & TP & Breakeven	33.9	5867	108	173	218	2.05

Graph showing equity curve by only using volatility stop-loss, take-profit and break-even, we got some smoother equity curve.

Trailing Stop

When we are using the trailing-stop below the previous lower high, we have some distance below the low of that candle. I will also introduce this distance between previous lower high and stop-loss as function of recent volatility. In essence we don't have a stop-loss, we allow the trailing-stop to do the work, with this we saw the following results:

Method	Average profit	Sum Profit	# of winning trades	# of total trades	Standard deviation	Rel number
SL & TP	26.0	4497	98	173	234	1.46
SL & TP & Breakeven	33.9	5867	108	173	218	2.05
Trailing stop	87.4	15119	68	173	370	3.11
Trailing stop + Breakeven	95.8	16572	90	173	360	3.50

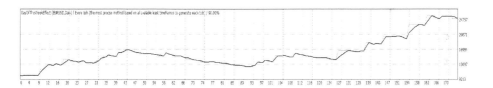

Graph showing equity curve with only trailing-stop

Graph showing equity curve with only trailing-stop and break-even

We see that by using trailing-stop we nearly tripled our average return, but we get less winning trades because, but overall increased our total profit to 15,119 also Rel number increased to 3.11 which is improvement. Then we introduced a break-even function where we locked in some profits after the market moved, this is also a function of volatility. We increased our profit and Rel number to 3.5, a noticeable difference. The last time we introduced break-even we got worse results than when we kept it out. This time when break-even is a function of volatility we got better results. However, what is more important is the out of sample results.

Out of Sample Test

We have been refining the strategy and the aim is to optimize it on in sample data and get good out of sample data. Out of sample data is 01.01.2012–01.09.2016.

Method	Average profit	Sum Profit	# of winning trades	# of total trades	Standard deviation	Rel number
SL & TP	26.0	4497	98	173	234	1.46
SL & TP & Breakeven	33.9	5867	108	173	218	2.05
Trailing stop	87.4	15119	68	173	370	3.11
Trailing stop + Breakeven	95.8	16572	90	173	360	3.50
Out of sample test	37.3	1232	20	33	185	1.16

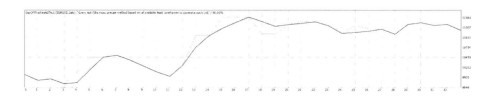

Graph showing out of sample test

We got a sum profit of 1,232 and Rel number for 1.16, and 20 of the 33 trades were profitable. Actually, I'm satisfied with the results because the pair even though it had a downtrend at the start of 2014, it ended up ranging towards the end of the year. This uptrend strategy remained on the same levels during a range bound period which is good. More often than not, in the instances where the market goes from one sentiment to another, people usually experience huge losses. We however remained mostly level with only small drawdowns.

Summary

There is not much more to change or adjust on this method. It is time for us to decide whether or not the Day of The Week Effect strategy can be used. My conclusion is that it can be used and is still valid but not with the old way that traders have used it to manage trades. You should use break-evens and lock in some profit when the trade has moved your way. We saw that when we did not account for volatility, we got much better in sample results. We then lost all of our money in the out of sample period, when not accounting for the volatility. But when we optimized accounting for the volatility we got acceptable out of sample results.

I would not recommend to anyone putting all their money on one pair. It is essential that you diversify your risk amongst uncorrelated currency pairs and uncorrelated securities. Therefore if one pair is ranging, not making much money or taking a loss, the other will be in an uptrend. Your losses in the ranging pair or security will be offset by your larger profits from the currency/security which is in a trend. I ran this strategy trying to buy on different days*Monday, Tuesday, etc., used the same settings for managing the trade, I also received the result that Friday was the best day to buy in an up-trending market for the test.

CHAPTER 4:
What Are Realistic Profits To Target In The Market?

When many people begin trading, myself included, we are often told that it is a good way to make money within a short period of time. I developed some strategies and they did well to begin with but had they also included huge drawdowns. With these types of results it is easy for one to conclude there must have been something wrong with the strategy. At one point I had 20 % percent returns a month, which meant that I was doubling my capital within six months. In some months I even had 30% returns.

As good as the returns were, the dramatic drawdowns were a sign that things were far from perfect. I then went off on a mission in an attempt to discover what were the limits and what were realistic returns. Where to begin? should I read forums? Not really, they are usually filled with unvetted people bragging of doubling of their accounts in one month etc. without providing you access to their trade data. Unfortunately, even the trade data can be falsified.

I wanted to find out how other professionals were doing, comparing my results against the results of the institutional traders. These are the people who are paid generous salaries and bonuses to make money by trading/investing for the big investment funds and banks.

To accomplish my research goals, there are useful tools like the Barclay Currency Traders Index and the Barclay Systematic Traders Index. They track the results of more than 400 long term audited systematic and manual currency traders.

Systematic Traders

Year	Return	Year	Return	Year	Return
1980	-	1993	8.19%	2006	2.10%
1981	-	1994	-3.18%	2007	8.72%
1982	-	1995	15.27%	2008	18.16%
1983	-	1996	11.58%	2009	-3.38%
1984	-	1997	12.76%	2010	7.82%
1985	-	1998	8.12%	2011	-3.83%
1986	-	1999	-3.71%	2012	-3.20%
1987	63.01%	2000	9.89%	2013	-1.10%
1988	12.22%	2001	2.99%	2014	10.32%
1989	1.18%	2002	12.09%	2015	-2.92%
1990	34.58%	2003	8.71%	2016	0.32%[†]
1991	13.37%	2004	0.54%		
1992	3.25%	2005	0.95%		

[†]Estimated YTD performance for 2016 calculated with reported data as of October-21-2016 12:08 US CST

At a Glance from Jan 1987

Compound Annual Return	7.56%
Sharpe Ratio	0.34
Worst Drawdown	22.07%
Correlation vs S&P 500	-0.04
Correlation vs US Bonds	0.11
Correlation vs World Bonds	-0.04

The compounded yearly profits since 1987 is 7,56%

The Currency Traders

At a Glance from Jan 1987

Compound Annual Return	6.54%
Sharpe Ratio	0.32
Worst Drawdown	15.26%
Correlation vs S&P 500	-0.02
Correlation vs US Bonds	0.13
Correlation vs World Bonds	-0.02

Year	Return	Year	Return	Year	Return
1980	-	1993	-3.33%	2006	-0.12%
1981	-	1994	-5.96%	2007	2.59%
1982	-	1995	11.49%	2008	3.50%
1983	-	1996	6.69%	2009	0.91%
1984	-	1997	11.35%	2010	3.45%
1985	-	1998	5.71%	2011	2.25%
1986	-	1999	3.12%	2012	1.71%
1987	29.56%	2000	4.45%	2013	0.87%
1988	4.28%	2001	2.71%	2014	3.35%
1989	18.89%	2002	6.29%	2015	4.65%
1990	57.74%	2003	11.08%	2016	0.25%[†]
1991	10.94%	2004	2.36%		
1992	10.27%	2005	-1.21%		

[†]Estimated YTD performance for 2016 calculated with reported data as of October 21-2016 12:08 US CST

The currency traders have experienced 6,54% compounded yearly profits since 1987.

The best fund had Profit/maximum drawdown of 1 but the average was on 0.5 for all of the funds. This means that the "big boys" also experienced drawdowns which were twice the returns. With a long-term view they were in profit overall.

CHAPTER 5:
Short Term Fast Growth vs Long Term Slow Growth

We will examine two ways of operating in the market, short term with fast growth and long term with slow growth. The driver behind fast growth is the high leverage that traders have access to in the markets. This leverage allows you to trade with much more market exposure than the funds that you have available in an account. This also means that you can open yourself to additional risks, some may even say that you are gambling. The risk of a total loss of capital can be high. The increased risk is coupled the opportunity to have faster growth. The second approach is to develop strategies that gives you smaller profits while at the same time having lower risk.

The first approach (fast and high-risk) is considered by many to be gambling with your capital and regularly has a high rate of failure. Success, when it does occur is largely due to random luck and usually does not last for a significant period of time. There is only a small percentage of people who attempt fast and high-risk that gain any financial rewards.

Some of the individuals who do achieve significant profits through their initial high-risk ventures, leverage their success to live from that capital by later trading lower risk methods. However, as stated, the risk of a total loss of capital is high and the probabilities of success are low. I suggest that you strive to build capital gradually with a low drawdown strategy to keep the losses small.

Forex trading is about making calculated trades while keeping capital preservation and risk management in mind. Your initial aim is surviving in the market. Survival is one of the most important things for a trader and the reason why capital preservation should be executed in an aggressive manner. Controlling risk should be a priority before aiming for profits. You need to consider more of how you will avoid losing money to the market than how much capital you want to take out. As I say in the classes that I teach "make failure survivable." With this base and understanding that you have we can move towards the next set of strategies.

You can check Barclays Indices here:

http://www.barclayhedge.com/research/indices/cta/sub/sys.html

CHAPTER 6:
The Big Boys VS Small Traders

I n this chapter I will reveal more insights about the financial markets, especially the differences between the average small trader and the institutions.

Averaging The Price Doesn't Make Sense

When I first began working as a trader it was common to hear "averaging the price." Initially it sounded odd and didn't make much sense to me. Why should people buy more of a security if it was falling? Just try to think about it as a rational person, would you invest more money where you are already experiencing losses? No, and it doesn't make any sense either to the average investor. We were also told "cut your losses and let your profit run", and that is a very good trading strategy. Another of the early lessons was that we should have at least a 1:2 risk/reward ratio. It is in our nature as opportunists, we usually prefer to bet when the expectation of gain is more in our favor. This is especially true when we know that the money we are investing we will at least double them when we are right, and lose less if we are wrong. Even a fool with only one banana doesn't want to bet it if he knows it will not return at least two, we want double of the amount we are risking.

Nothing Is Free, You Even Have to Pay For Water

When you find a good recipe, and if followed step by step you should have a tasty cake or a delicious dish in front of you. You were told that if followed exactly you would get this result. In a similar manner what we traders/investors do is we believe that if we read books, or watch videos and simply follow those instructions we will get a solid plan which will help us become successful. However, what we are forgetting, which is sometimes stated in these sources, is that we pay to learn trading. The profits do not come without risk. You have to risk a certain amount of money to get money from the market. You will read about the traditional 1:2 risk to reward ratio. What they are offering you is a cost of the book to wealth ratio. It is unlikely that someone will give away their complete trading strategies on how to become a millionaire or billionaire in a 25 dollar book while teaching you to have a 1:2 risk/reward ratio. It is not the full story, the 1:2 ratio has its merits, but no one will do that trade with you, even the smiling fool will refuse your offer of 25 Dollars if he knows some get rich quick strategy that *actually* works. Another reason why NO claims of instant riches are made anywhere in this book.

In the markets it is you against the rest of the trading world, the chances of winning are best for the most prepared. When you earn money, someone on the other side is losing some, it is not like earning profits on fruits that you are harvesting. Remember that you are taking money out of someone's pocket and they will *not* allow that to happen easily. Even withdrawing your own funds from a bank has a fee now a days, and yes you even pay for water which is a free natural source.

Solution to the problem

Let us suppose you used 4 years of your spare time, weekends and nights to become a successful trader. You read every book that you could possibly think about. Read numerous online sources that should help you to become successful, but nothing helped. Then you begin to think about what could be wrong with your approach when it seems that others are getting it right. A crucial mistake in judgement was to trust blindly some of the literature written about investing. After some thought you would have concluded that nothing is free and if it exist it is too good to be true. This was the experience of a trader friend of mine. He then started adding philosophy books to his reading list. Philosophers are critical thinkers, it helped him to become critical and think differently, which are great qualities to have as a trader.

As I remember, my friend does not even trust doctors. For many people, doctors are one of the professions that they trust the most. You would probably trust a doctor more than a banker. That impulse of trust is not as straight forward as you would think. Health literature, like financial literature is also based on empirical studies and findings where you have a hypothesis that you try to reject or prove significant. You attempt to link a cause and result, if you do A then B will happen. Keep in mind these studies, in noticeable numbers, are exposed to a lot of randomness which the authors probably have tried to "sell" you or by fitting a theory to the results. This reminds me of the saying: "If you torture the data enough, it will confess". Also in these studies there is a 5% chance that the results may be wrong or not significant. The lesson is to be more thorough and not accept information without a rational assessment prior to making your decision.

To reinforce my point, you should try to buy a stock (on a demo account) the next time a financial newspaper has information about increased earnings reported by a listed company. This will provide a practical understanding of what I am writing about. I have seen many times that a stock plunges after such "good" news. Who pays the bill? the average investor, who makes the money? the professionals of course, that is why I recommend this practice of thinking critically and learn from people who are trading. For example, Warren Buffet is known for making good investment decisions which you also could copy but you need to have the same objectives that he has. He is a long term value investor.

The Unpleasant Truth

This truth relates to how professional hedge and pension funds trade their money. For those seeking or needing another perspective on this I suggest that you watch the movie "The Big Short." If you do not have time for the full movie you can watch the trailers on YouTube to get an idea of what it is about. In the film, the big investment funds sold and sold even more when their initial positions were experiencing losses. These market players were able to hold their positions because they borrowed money for the margin requirements. In the movie they detailed how these people made billions of dollars in the last financial crisis. They were initially short and when the market went higher they shorted even more at the higher price, by the way, they did not use a stop-loss.

More on stop-losses. Investors like a Warren Buffet do not operate in the world of stop-losses. They do not look to exit on the drop in price of a long position. Buffet and institutional traders are not using stop-losses and they can afford not to because they have deep pockets. Investment funds can remain in a losing trade for a long time because it is just a small part of their larger portfolio and they have available an almost unimaginable amount of capital for the margin requirements.

This is from an article in "Marketwatch" telling that Buffet bought even more on a sell off:

Warren Buffett showed that the sell off in Wells Fargo & Co.'s stock this year has just made him love the banking giant even more, as he boosted his stake in the company to 504.3 million shares, according to regulatory filings.

Wells Fargo's WFC, -0.23% stock dropped 1.3% on Tuesday, which suggests Buffett has lost about $327.8 million on his stake on the day.

Link to the article: http://www.marketwatch.com/story/warren-buffett-buys-more-wells-fargo-stock-on-a-dip-2016-03-29

The guru was able to have an open position running a loss of $327.7 million, instead of showing any signs of concern he went on to increase his stake. The average investor would have difficulty keeping a cool head with a losing position of a few thousand dollars (USD). Hopefully the difference is becoming clearer now. Allow me to explain further on how things are vastly different when an average investor trades and when the big institutions are trading.

Average Trader:
He will open a long position in a security with too much risk of his total portfolio. Our trader knows that if this security falls below a certain amount it will hurt his account and he will be stopped out. Also if he does not close the position, there will be insufficient capital for further trades. To avoid this scenario the stop-loss is executed and a loss is

taken on the trade. Our investor finds a new security and he rinses and repeat the strategy.

<u>The Big Boys:</u>

They have a trade plan, they typically have just a small portion of their portfolio invested in a single security and they have an exit strategy. They have also done a "what if" analysis of their trade before they opened it. If they are long and the security falls it's a potential jackpot for them. These institutions get to buy more at a lower price, then buy again, maybe even double of their initial position. If everything goes wrong and the broker gives a margin call, they just borrow money from their network or negotiate the margin requirements.

What are most (not all), smaller and inexperienced traders unable to do? first, is to borrow huge sums of money with ease, second, which make things worse, they usually do not have an exit strategy or a trade plan. Many just want to open a trade without even giving it much thought.

CHAPTER 7:
The Martingale Strategy Explained

H ere I will highlight and explain a technique that has made amazing profits over the span of 5-6 years in our test. The results are revealed near the end of the chapter!

The strategy that we will examine is called Martingale. Basically, it requires that you increase your lot size and buy more when your initial position is in the red. You do need to have some distance between the orders in order to give your trade some room. By the way, this strategy is also used by gamblers, just to provide full disclosure and warning.

This Martingale technique has been one of my interest for some time, but it was difficult to fully grasp the technique by manual trading alone. Therefore my colleague and I wrote a script and created an algorithm. We had an entry signal which was actually bad and in addition we had a take-profit. The timeframe used was 30 minutes and the lot size was 0.01, with a starting balance of 10,000 USD.

After the initial trade was executed we placed 5 sell limit pending orders above our entry signal.

You can see on the graph that one of the pending orders was triggered and quickly after it closed both orders at break-even.

Here is another example of our strategy.

Here we have two closing mechanisms one is used only if the initial order opened, this is the strategy trigger, another one is used if one of the pending orders is triggered then we will close when we have total open profit of 0, or break-even. You can see adding to a losing position is used as backup if we were wrong. I did not optimize anything, the test pair was EURUSD and the period was 01.01.2010–10.26.2010.

We got following results:

	Average profit	Sum profit	Winning trade	Total trades	Standard dev	Relnumber
0.1 Startoning lot	45	20066	244	450	307	3
0.9 Starting lot	401	180598	244	450	2763	3
0.9 Starting lot and stoploss	207	86784	227	419	2710	1.6

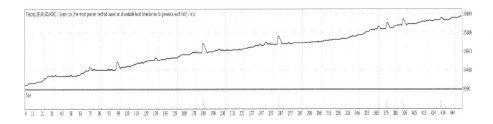

0.1 starting lot size

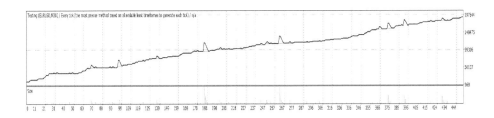

0.9 starting lot size

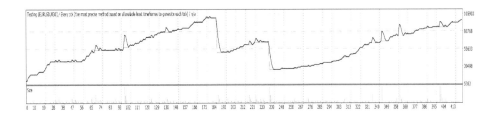

With stop-loss order instead of fifth pending order

We ran a backtest as low and high-risk. In the low-risk your initial trade has a lot size of 0.1 and with the high-risk test your initial lot size is higher as 0.9. With 0.1 we had around a 200 % return during a 5 year time period, averaging 40 % yearly return and with the high-risk you have even better returns during the 5 year period. You are able to see that the equity curve increased linearly which is also good, you don't experience a drawdown.

What if we also included a safety net to prevent a total account wipe out? What I did was have 4 pending orders and the last pending order was changed with a stop-loss order meaning above that level all open orders would have been closed. I saw a smaller profit but we had an increase of 800% since 2010. You also see from the graph that we had some big drawdowns, for me is this a good strategy rather than adjusting another one to only make average money. I am comfortable with a certain amount of risk, but I would have not risked more than 10,000 USD if I wanted to invest in this strategy.

Summary

We see that if we wish to trade like the big banks then we need to throw out the stop-loss using mentality. When institutions are in a buy mode of a security they are *really* long and if the security goes down then they simply purchase more of it at a lower level. They will rarely if ever use a stop-loss. They operate without stops because they can. What smaller traders can risk is a margin call or a stop-out if the security never retraces. What we can do is maybe using stop-loss in addition, where you only place 4 sell limit orders but if the price increases even further we just close all our orders and take the loss. If I were a passive investor

I would prefer this technique than to always get stop hunted by the brokers and lose out on trades. This strategy should be considered, but preferably with low risk, small lot sizes and as part of a broader portfolio. Have a look at the steady growth of the equity curve, we never had a drawdown which is a good sign to make money as the big traders do.

CHAPTER 8:
Adding To Winners – How Professionals Manage Their Trades

A s we have seen the Martingale strategy is simply buying even more when the market goes against you. There is also another strategy called the Anti-martingale. To execute this you will double or triple your investment when you are in profit. In our scenario, you entered the market and are long a stock with an entry price of $50. You also have a predefined rule that if the market moves up to $55 you will move the stop-loss of the first trade to break-even and open another trade with double the lot size. Your target price for both trades will be $60.

The advantage of the strategy is that if you are correct you will make much more money than you lose when you are wrong. The market does not have to move so much, because you have increased your trading amount. This is known as "adding to the winners." The disadvantage is that if the market reverses after triggering you second or your fifth order, you are now trading with additional orders and will experience larger losses.

Scenario 1								
Trades	Amount		Price		SL	TP		Result
1	0.0100		1.5610		1.5600	1.5590		-10
Total								-10
Scenario 2								
Trades	Amount		Price		SL	TP		Result
1	0.0100		1.5610		1.5600	1.5590		0
2	0.0300		1.5600		1.5610	1.5590		-30
Total								-30
Scenario 3								
Trades	Amount		Price		SL	TP		Result
1	0.0100		1.5610		1.5600	1.5590		20
2	0.0300		1.5600		1.5610	1.5590		30
Total								50

Scenario 1: Only the first trade is triggered and stop-loss is activated if we have a loss of -10.

Scenario 2: Both trades are triggered, but stop-loss of the first trade is changed to break-even, but if the stop-loss of the second is triggered we get loss of -30.

Scenario 3: Both trades are triggered, and both reaches take profit we get total profit of 50.

Entry Signal

If we have a high above Bollinger bands and the candle after it close below previous close, we open a short trade. (see chart)

Trade Management

If the price goes above 100 pips we close the trade. If the price goes below 100 pips from the entry price we open a second trade with double of the amount as first trade and we also change stop-loss of the first trade to break-even. Stop-loss of the second trade is same as the entry price of the first trade, which is 100 pips. Both positions have take-profit 200 pips from where we entered the first trade. We used a volatility based distance, our distance between the orders is a function of the daily volatility. This is important because, as mentioned before, the volatility is different at different times.

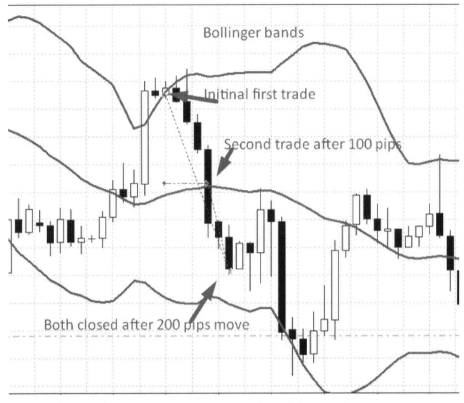

Picture above illustrates our entry signal and the trade management.

Test instrument: EURUSD

Test period: 01.01.2009–01.01.2016

Starting balance: 10,000 USD

Timeframe: 4 Hour chart

Test results:

Average profit	Sum profit	Winning trade	Total trades	Standard dev	Relnumber
27	8949	140	330	206	2

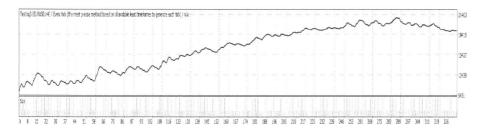

During a period of 7 years we had around 90% profit, of total 330 trades 140 were profitable trades. You see that equity curve also increases steadily which is good, we have some losses and some wins, but on average we make money.

Summary

We can conclude that this trade management tool is a good way to deal with trades that do not have a good winning profile. One can also see from the equity curve that we don't experience any huge drawdowns. The key is that you must ensure that the distance between your orders are a function of volatility. This strategy should be considered if you are seeking an alternative to the traditional 1:2 or 1:3 risk to reward ratio. Many professional traders use this strategy with much success in their trade.

CONCLUSION

Thank you for making it through to the end *Expert Advisor And Forex Trading Strategies*. Let's hope it was informative and that it was able to provide you with the some additional tools that will help you achieve your trading goals. The next steps, as I always recommend in my books is to take action. Set up a demo account with your favorite trading provider and test the strategies until you achieve the results that you need to see before opening a live account.

My others books that have been proven to assist traders and investors are: *Technical Analysis for Forex Explained* and *Expert Advisor Programming for Beginners: Maximum MT4 Forex Profit Strategies.*

PROFILE OF THE AUTHOR

Wayne Walker is the director of a global capital markets education and consulting firm (gcmsonline.info). He has several years experience in leading and coaching teams of Investment Advisors and has managed top performing teams in the Private Client Group based on Bench Mark Earnings (BME).

Made in United States
Troutdale, OR
03/15/2024

18503504R00038